In My Own Words

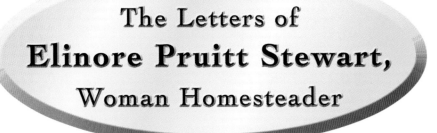

The Letters of
Elinore Pruitt Stewart,
Woman Homesteader

Edited by Ruth Ashby
Illustrations by Laszlo Kubinyi

BENCHMARK BOOKS

MARSHALL CAVENDISH
NEW YORK

With thanks to Dr. Susanne K. George, editor of The Adventures of
the Woman Homesteader: The Life and Letters of Elinore Pruitt Stewart
*(University of Nebraska Press, 1992), for her generous assistance in
providing the photograph of Elinore.*

Benchmark Books
Marshall Cavendish
99 White Plains Road
Tarrytown, New York 10591-9001
www.marshallcavendish.com

Library of Congress Cataloging-in-Publication Data

Stewart, Elinore Pruitt, 1878-
  The letters of Elinore Pruitt Stewart, woman homesteader / edited by
Ruth Ashby.
    p. cm. — (In my own words)
Summary: Presents the diary of a woman who made a life for herself and her daughter by
homesteading in Wyoming in the early years of the twentieth century.
  ISBN 0-7614-1645-5
  1. Stewart, Elinore Pruitt, 1878—Correspondence. 2. Women pioneers—Wyoming—
Correspondence. 3. Pioneers—Wyoming—Correspondence. 4. Frontier and pioneer
life—Wyoming. 5. Wyoming--Biography. [1. Stewart, Elinore Pruitt, 1878 Correspondence.
2. Women pioneers—Wyoming. 3. Pioneers—Wyoming. 4. Frontier and pioneer life—
Wyoming. 5. Women—Biography. 6. Wyoming—History--20th century.] I. Title. II.
Series: In my own words (Benchmark Books (Firm))

  F761.S8 2003
  978.7'85—dc21

                        2003000973

ISBN: 0-7614-1645-5

Printed in China

1 3 5 6 4 2

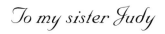

To my sister Judy

Elinore on her ranch

Elinore's Book

Introduction

In late March 1909, a wagon rumbled into the tiny frontier town of Burntfork, Wyoming. Its passengers, Elinore Pruitt Rupert and her two-year-old daughter, Jerrine, had traveled all the way from Denver, Colorado, and were tired and dusty from the long trip. But they were excited, too. They were starting a new life on the range, and this isolated community on the Utah-Wyoming border would be their home.

Eager for a fresh start, Elinore had agreed to be housekeeper for a cattle rancher named Clyde Stewart. She figured that once she had a chance to pick out some land, she, like Clyde, could acquire a homestead from the U.S. government. According to the Homestead Act of 1862, anyone who lived on and improved 160 acres of western land for five years could keep it. Ranching was backbreaking—and often heartbreaking—work. But Elinore believed she had the grit, stamina, and determination to succeed. Her dream was to be a woman homesteader.

Over the course of the next four years, Elinore wrote a series of letters back to a friend in Denver that described the challenges she faced. By turns humorous, touching, and exciting, the letters tell the fascinating story of Elinore's "home on the range." Her friend, a retired schoolteacher from Boston named Juliet Coney, recognized their literary value and contacted the popular

Atlantic Monthly magazine about publication. The letters were first published in the magazine as a series in 1913–1914 and then as a book, *Letters of a Woman Homesteader.* They earned immediate popularity. Elinore, readers felt, was a genuine woman of the American West: courageous, resilient, and independent.

Elinore Pruitt was born on June 3, 1876, in what is now the state of Oklahoma, the oldest of nine children. The family was so poor she didn't even have shoes until she was six years old. Her one brief educational experience was cut short when her teacher was hanged for stealing a horse. For the rest of her life Elinore read widely, trying to make up for her lack of formal education. When she was a teenager, Elinore's parents died within a year of each other, and her hard life became harder. As the oldest child, Elinore tried to keep her family together and raise her siblings. When she was about twenty-six, she married a man named Harry Rupert, with whom she had a daughter, Jerrine, in 1906. The marriage ended in divorce, and Elinore went west in search of better opportunities. It was while working as a housekeeper and nurse (she called herself a "washlady") for kind Mrs. Coney in Denver that Elinore came up with the idea of homesteading. And that is where our story begins.

Wyoming in 1909 was a wilderness of sweeping plains, majestic canyons, and craggy mountains. Even today it is the least populated state in the nation; in 1909 it had only 150,000 people. It was easy to get lost in such wide-open spaces. No wonder Elinore felt that every human contact was precious. Her letters are full of stories about all the unusual people she met: the ranchers, the hired hands, the wives, and the widows. There is Mrs. Louderer, the indomitable German widow whose son was killed in a freak accident and who ended up running a ranch by herself. Zebulon Pike Parker, the eccentric old man who came west searching for gold and still cherished memories of his boyhood sweetheart back in Arkansas. Star Crosby, the sweet baby born in a logging camp and named for the bright night sky.

Above all, there was Elinore herself, always delightful, always ready for another adventure. Other people might have been soured by such a hard life. But her own troubles merely made Elinore more sympathetic to the difficulties of others. In true frontier fashion, she was always ready to lend a helping hand to neighbors in need. They, in turn, were happy to help her.

It isn't giving anything away to reveal that Elinore married Clyde Stewart, the taciturn rancher. (She loved to make fun of his Scottish accent.) She was thirty-three, and he was forty-one. It was a marriage undertaken partly as a matter of convenience, but it evolved into a partnership of great loyalty and affection. Together they raised Jerrine and three sons, Clyde Jr., Calvin, and Robert, and managed two homesteads, his and hers. They still owned their ranch twenty-four years later, when Elinore died following surgery, at age fifty-seven.

The most amazing thing about Elinore is simply how much she did. Milking cows, mowing hay, baking bread, growing corn, raising children, nursing friends and family, and writing—at times she truly seems like the Wonder

Woman of the West. Yet her hard work did not make Elinore exceptional. The women and men who risked everything to settle the West all worked without ceasing. What set Elinore apart was her almost endless optimism and energy. Even today, Elinore's letters radiate the joy, hope, and vitality with which she lived her life.

Here then, is Elinore Pruitt Stewart in her own words.

—Ruth Ashby
Huntington, New York

The Letters of
Elinore Pruitt Stewart,
Woman Homesteader

The road, being so muddy, was full of ruts, and the stage acted as if it had the hiccoughs.

Arrival at Burnt Fork

Burnt Fork, Wyoming,
April 18, 1909

Dear Mrs. Coney, —

Are you thinking I am lost, like the Babes in the Wood? Well, I am not. I am 'way up close to the Forest Reserve of Utah, within half a mile of the line, sixty miles from the railroad. I was twenty-four hours on the train and two days on the stage, and oh, those two days! The snow was just beginning to melt and the mud was about the worst I ever heard of.

The road, being so muddy, was full of ruts, and the stage acted as if it had the hiccoughs. Once Mr. Stewart [her new employer] asked me if I did not think it a "gey duir trip." I told him he could call it gay if he wanted to, but it didn't seem very hilarious to me.

At last we "arriv," and everything is just lovely for me. I have a very very comfortable situation and Mr. Stewart is absolutely no trouble, for as soon as he has his meals he retires to his room and plays on his bagpipe, only he calls it his "bugpeep."

There is a saddle horse especially for me and a little shotgun with which I am to kill sage chickens. We are between two trout streams, so you can think of me as being happy when the snow is through melting and the water gets clear. We have the finest flock of Plymouth

Rocks and get so many nice eggs. It sure seems fine to have all the cream I want after my town experiences. Jerrine is making good use of all the good things we are having. She rides the pony to work every day.

I have not filed on my land yet because the snow is fifteen feet deep on it, and I think I would rather see what I am getting, so will wait until summer. They have just three seasons here, winter and July and August. We are to plant our garden the last of May.

Please write me when you have time.

Sincerely yours,
Elinore Rupert

Filing a Claim

Dear, Dear Mrs. Coney, —

Well, I have filed on my land and am now a landowner. I have filed adjoining Mr. Stewart and I am well pleased. I have a grove of twelve swamp pines on my place, and I am going to build my house there. I thought it would be very romantic to live on the peaks amid the whispering pines, but I reckon it would be powerfully uncomfortable also.

A neighbor and his daughter were going to Green River, the county-seat, and said I might go along, so I did. I could file there as well as at the land office. And oh, that trip! It took us a whole week to go and come. We camped out, of course, for in the whole sixty miles there was but one house.

The sagebrush is so short in some places that it is not large enough to make a fire, so we had to drive until quite late before we camped [for the] night. We came about sundown to a beautiful canyon. In the canyon the shadows had already fallen, but when we looked up we could see the last shafts of sunlight on the tops of the great bare buttes.

Suddenly a great wolf started from somewhere and galloped along the edge of the canyon, outlined black and clear by the setting sun. His curiosity overcame him at last,

HOMESTEADING

In 1862 Congress passed the Homestead Act. It offered 160 acres of land to anyone who would live on the land for five years, improve it, and pay a small filing fee. Hundreds of thousands of people flocked to the government land offices to take advantage of the opportunity. They settled on the Great Plains to farm wheat and corn. Others established cattle ranches in areas stretching from Kansas north to Colorado, Wyoming, and Montana. The new settlers faced blizzards in winter; drought, grass fires, and swarms of grasshoppers in summer. The most discouraged went back east. Those hoping for a more congenial climate kept going west to the Pacific. The ones who stayed saw the growth of towns and, eventually, the end of the American frontier. By 1900 the plains were home to half a million farmers.

In the beginning, most of those who took up the challenge of homesteading were men. But by 1910, 10 percent of homesteaders were women. Some had been widowed or, like Elinore, divorced. Others were single women looking for independence and a chance to support themselves. They found hard work and, sometimes, adventure.

so he sat down and waited to see what manner of beast we were. I reckon he was disappointed for he howled most dismally.

After we quitted the canyon I saw the most beautiful sight. It seemed as if we were driving through a golden haze. The violet shadows were creeping up between the hills, while away back of us the snow-capped peaks were catching the sun's last rays. On every side of us stretched the poor, hopeless desert, the sage, grim and determined to live in spite of starvation, and the great, bare, desolate buttes. The beautiful colors turned to amber and rose, and then to the general tone, dull gray.

Then we stopped to camp, and such a scurrying around to gather brush for the fire and to get supper! Everything tasted so good! Jerrine ate like a man. Then we raised the wagon tongue and spread the wagon sheet over it and made a bedroom for us women. We made our beds on the warm, soft sand and went to bed.

Well, I must quit writing before you vote me a nuisance. With lots of love to you,

Your sincere friend,
Elinore Rupert

A Busy, Happy Summer

Dear Mrs. Coney, —

This has been for me the busiest, happiest summer I can remember. I have worked very hard, but it has been work that I really enjoy. Help of any kind is very hard to get here, and Mr. Stewart had been too confident of getting men, so that haying caught him with too few men to put up the hay. He had no man to run the mower and he couldn't run both the mower and the stacker, so you can fancy what a place he was in.

I don't know that I ever told you, but my parents died within a year of each other and left six of us to shift for ourselves. Our people offered to take one here and there among them until we should all have a place, but we refused to be raised on the halves and so arranged to stay at Grandmother's and keep together. Well, we had no money to hire men to do our work, so had to learn to do it ourselves. Consequently I learned to do many things which girls more fortunately situated don't even know have to be done.

Among the things I learned to do was the way to run a mowing machine. It cost me many bitter tears because I got sunburned, and my hands were hard, rough, and stained with machine oil. I used to wonder how any Prince Charming could overlook all that in any girl he came to. Well, when my prince showed up I wrapped my hands in my old checked apron and took him up before he could catch his breath. Then there was no more mowing, and I almost forgot that I knew how until Mr. Stewart got into such a panic. I was afraid to tell him I could mow for fear he would forbid me to do so.

But one morning, when he was chasing a last hope of help, I went down to the barn, took out the horses, and went to mowing. I had enough cut before he got back to show him I knew how. As he came back manless he was delighted as well as surprised. I was glad because I really like to mow, and besides that, I am adding feathers to my cap in a surprising way. When you see me again you will think I am wearing a feather duster. But it is only that I have been said to have almost as much sense as a "mon," and that is an honor I never aspired to, even in my wildest dreams.

I have done most of my cooking at night, have milked seven cows every day, and have done all the hay-cutting, so you see I have been working. But I have found time to put up thirty pints of jelly and the same amount of jam for myself. I used wild fruits, gooseberries, currants, raspberries, and cherries. I have almost two gallons of the cherry butter, and I think it is delicious. I wish I could get some of it to you. I am sure you would like it.

Sincerely yours,
Elinore Rupert

P.S. MR. STEWART IS GOING TO PUT UP MY HOUSE FOR ME IN PAY FOR MY EXTRA WORK.

I AM ASHAMED OF MY LONG LETTERS TO YOU, BUT I AM SUCH A MURDERER OF LANGUAGE THAT I HAVE TO USE IT ALL TO TELL ANYTHING.

PLEASE DON'T ENTIRELY FORGET ME. YOUR LETTERS MEAN SO MUCH TO ME AND I WILL TRY TO ANSWER MORE PROMPTLY.

A Charming Adventure

September 28, 1909

Dear Mrs. Coney, —

Your second card just reached me and I am plumb glad because, although I answered your other, I was wishing I could write you, for I have had the most charming adventure.

All the men left for the round-up, to be gone a week. I knew I never could stand myself a whole week. I got reckless and determined to do something real bad. So I went down to the barn and saddled Robin Adair, placed a pack on "Jeems McGregor," then Jerrine and I left for a camping-out expedition.

It was nine o'clock when we started and we rode hard until about four, when I turned Robin loose, saddle and all, for I knew he would go home. I put Jerrine on the pack and led Jeems for about two hours longer; then, as I had come to a good place to camp, we stopped.

We had been climbing higher into the mountains all day and had reached a level tableland where the grass was luxuriant and there was plenty of wood and water. I unpacked Jeems and staked him out, built a roaring fire, and made our bed in an angle of a sheer wall of rock where we would be protected against the wind. Then I put some potatoes into the embers, as baby and I are both fond of roasted potatoes. I started to a little spring to get

I started to a little spring to get water for my coffee when I saw a couple of jack rabbits playing, so I went back for my little shotgun.

water for my coffee when I saw a couple of jack rabbits playing, so I went back for my little shotgun. I shot one of the rabbits. It was fat and young, and it was but the work of a moment to dress it and hang it up on a tree. Then I fried some slices of bacon, made myself a cup of coffee, and Jerrine and I sat on the ground and ate. Everything smelled and tasted so good! Presently we crept under our Navajos and, being tired, were soon asleep.

The sun was just gilding the hilltops when we arose. Everything, even the barrenness, was beautiful. We have had frosts, and the quaking aspens were a trembling field of gold as far up the stream as we could see. We were way up above them and could look far across the valley. We could see the silvery gold of the willows, the russet and bronze of the currants, and patches of cheerful green showed where the pines were.

That day was more toilsome than the last, but a very happy one. The meadowlarks kept singing like they were glad to see us. But we were still climbing and soon gone beyond the larks and sage chickens, and up into the timber, where there are lots of grouse. It was quite dusky among the trees long before night, but it was all so grand and awe-inspiring. Occasionally there was an opening through which we could see the snowy peaks, seemingly just beyond us, toward which we were headed. But when you get among such grandeur you get to feel how little you are and how foolish is human endeavor, except that which unites us with the mighty force called God.

[At five o'clock] we decided to camp. The trees were

immense. I was nervous and wanted one that would protect us against any possible attack. At last we found one growing in a crevice of what seemed to be a sheer wall of rock. Nothing could reach us on two sides, and in front I could make a log heap which would give us warmth and make us safe. I wish you could once sleep on the kind of bed we enjoyed that night. It was both soft and firm, with the clean spicy smell of the pine. The heat from our big fire came in and we were warm as toast.

I could hardly remember where I was when I awoke. I arose and my head came in violent contact with a snag that was not there when I went to bed. As soon as I peered out, the mystery was explained.

Such a snowstorm I never saw! The snow had pressed the branches down lower, hence my bumped head. And then I began to think how many kinds of idiot I was. Here I was thirty or forty miles from home, in the mountains where no one goes in the winter. I knew the snow got to be ten or fifteen feet deep.

At last I decided to take a little hunt and provide for the day. I left Jerrine happy with the towel rolled up into a baby, and went along the brow of the mountain for almost a mile. Then I happened to look down into the canyon that lay east of us and saw smoke. Presently I heard a dog bark, and I knew I was near a camp of some kind. I resolved to join them, so went back to break my own camp.

At last everything was ready and Jerrine and I both mounted. If you think there is much comfort, or even security, in riding a pack-horse in a snowstorm over mountains

WYOMING

No one knows when the first white people set foot on the land that would become Wyoming. By the 1810s and 1820s, mountain men were already trading furs with the Native Americans. Beginning in 1843, travelers on the Oregon Trail were crossing Wyoming on their way to the Far West. Soon, there were so many traders, gold prospectors, and soldiers in the area that the Indians and newcomers clashed. A war with the Lakota ended with the Fort Laramie Treaty of 1868. The Indians agreed to allow railroads to be built, and the U.S. government promised to set aside a large reservation in South Dakota. But soon thousands of prospectors looking for gold in the Black Hills encroached upon the reservation. Another war broke out, and once again the Indians lost their home.

Wyoming's rugged land had attracted few settlers until the building of the Transcontinental Railroad in the 1860s. Cities grew up along the train route: Cheyenne, Laramie, Rock Springs, Green River. In 1868 Wyoming became a territory. One of its first laws was to grant the vote to women. That made Wyoming the first place in the world where women could vote. When Wyoming applied for statehood in 1890, some members of Congress insisted it change its law. But Wyoming legislators stood firm: "We may stay out of the Union for 100 years," they told Congress, "but we will come in with our women!" Wyoming was admitted, and its women continued to vote.

where there is no road, you are plumb wrong. At last, after what seemed like hours, we came into a "clearing," with a small log house and a fireplace. A little old man came bustling out, chewing his tobacco so fast, and almost frantic about his suspenders, which it seemed he couldn't get adjusted.

As I rode up, he said, "Whither, friend?" I said, "Hither." Then he said, "Light, stranger, and look at your saddle." So I "lit" and looked, and then I asked him what part of the South he was from. He answered, "Yell County, by gum! The best place in the United States, or in the world, either." That was my introduction to Zebulon Pike Parker.

He was so small and so old, but so cheerful and so sprightly, and a real Southerner! He had a big, open fireplace with backlogs and andirons. How I enjoyed it all! How we feasted on some of the deer killed "yisteddy," and real corn-pone baked in a skillet down on the hearth. He was so full of happy recollections and had a few that were not so happy. He came west "jist arter the wah"* on some expedition and "jist stayed." He told me about his home life back in Yell County, and I feel that I know all the "young uns."

At last it came out that he had not heard from home since he left it. "Don't you ever write?" I asked. "No, I am not an eddicated man, although I started to school. But my mother was an eddicated woman, yes'm. She could both read and write. I have the Bible she give me yit."

That night he spread down a buffalo robe and two

*"the wah"—the Civil War (1861–1865)

bearskins before the fire for Jerrine and me. I spread blankets over them and put a sleepy, happy little girl to bed, for he had insisted on making molasses candy for her because they happened to be born on the same day of the month. And then he played the fiddle until almost one o'clock.

After breakfast [the next morning] we set out for home. We rode "Jeems" and Mr. Parker rode the other mule. Poor, lonely, childlike little man! He tried to tell me how glad he had been to entertain me. "Why," he said, "I was plumb glad to see you and right sorry to have you go."

I got home at twelve and found, to my joy, that none of the men had returned. With many apologies for this outrageous letter, I am

Your ex-Washlady,
Elinore Rupert

Sedalia and Regalia

November 22, 1909

My Dear Friend, —

I am making a wedding dress. Don't grin; it isn't mine, —worse luck! But I must begin at the beginning. Just after I wrote you before, there came a terrific storm. The snow was just whirling when I saw some one pass the window. I opened the door and in came the dumpiest little woman and two daughters. She said she was "Mis' Lane." She had heard there was a new stranger in the country, so she had brought her twin girls, Sedalia and Regalia, to be neighborly. I was powerful glad I had a pot roast and some baked beans.

There could be no two people more unlike than the sisters. Sedalia is really handsome, and she is thin. But she is vain, selfish, shallow, and conceited. Gale is not even pretty, but she is clean and she is honest. She does many little things that are not exactly polite, but she is good and true.

They both went to the barn with me to milk. Gale tucked up her skirts and helped me. She said, "I just love a stable, with its hay and comfortable, contented cattle. I never go into one without thinking of the little baby Christ. I almost expect to see a little red baby in the straw every time I peek into a manger."

Sedalia answered, "Well, for Heaven's sake, get out of the stable to preach. Who wants to stand among these smelly cows all day?"

They stayed with us almost a week. One day when Gale and I were milking she asked me to invite her to stay with me a month. [Then her mother] asked me if I could not find enough to keep Gale busy for a month or two. She went on to explain that Sedalia was expecting to be married and that Gale was so "common" she would really spoil the match. I was surprised and indignant, especially as Sedalia sat and listened so brazenly. So I said I thought Sedalia would need all the help she could get to get married and that I should be glad to have Gale visit me as long as she liked.

So Gale stayed on with me. One afternoon she had gone to the post-office when I saw Mr. Patterson ride up. Now, from something Gale had said I fancied that Bob Patterson must be the right man. We had a long chat and he told me frankly he wanted Gale, but that she didn't care for him, and that they kept throwing "that danged Sedalia" at him. I broke the news to him that Gale was staying with me. He fairly beamed.

So that night I left Gale to wash dishes and Bob to help her while I held Mr. Stewart a prisoner in the stable and questioned him regarding Patterson's prospects and habits. I found both all that need be. When we went to the house Mr. Stewart said, "Weel, when are you bairns gangin' to the kirk?"*

*"Well, when are you children going to the church?"

28

They left it to me, so I set Thanksgiving Day, and as there is no "kirk to gang to," we are going to have a justice of the peace and they are to be married here. We are going to have the dandiest dinner that I can cook. Mr. Stewart went to town next day for the wedding dress, the gayest plaid outside of Caledonia. Joy waves are radiating from this ranch and about Thanksgiving morning one will strike you.

With lots of love and happy wishes,

Your ex-Washlady,
Elinore Rupert

Zebulon Pike Visits His Old Home

December 28, 1909

Dear Mrs. Coney, —

Our Thanksgiving affair was the most enjoyable happening I can remember for a long time. Zebulon Pike Parker came, but I had as a bait for him two fat letters from home. As soon as I came back from his place I wrote to Mrs. Carter [Zebulon's sister] and trusted to luck for my letter to reach her. I told her all I could about her brother and how seldom he left his mountain home. The letters were addressed to me along with a cordial letter from Mrs. Carter asking me to see that he got them.

Well, a more delighted little man I am sure never lived. I read the letters over and over, and answers were hurried off. He was dreadfully homesick, but couldn't figure on how he could leave the "critters," or how he could trust himself on a train. Mr. Stewart became interested, and he is a very resourceful man. So an old Frenchman was found who had no home and wanted a place to stay so he could trap. He was installed at Zebulon Pike's with full instructions as to each "critter's" peculiarities and needs.

Then one of the boys [one of Mr. Stewart's ranch hands], who was going home for Christmas to Memphis, was induced to wait for Mr. Parker and to see him safe to Little Rock. Mr. Stewart saw that he was properly clothed and made comfortable for the trip. Then he sent a telegram

30

to Judge Carter, who met Zebulon Pike at Little Rock, and they had a family reunion in Yell County.

I have had some charming letters from there. But that only proves what I have always said, that I am the luckiest woman in finding really lovely people and having really happy experiences. Good things are constantly happening to me. I wish I could tell you about my happy Christmas. But one of my New Year's resolutions was to stop loading you down with two-thousand-word letters.

I do hope this New Year may bring to you the desire of your heart and all that those who love you best most wish for you.

With lots and lots of love from baby and myself.

Your ex-Washlady,
Elinore Rupert

A Happy Christmas

Dear Mrs. Coney, —

My happy Christmas resulted from the ex-sheriff of this county being snowbound here. It seems that persons who come from a lower altitude to this country frequently become bewildered, especially if in poor health, leave the train at any stop and wander off into the hills. The ex-sheriff cited a case, that of a young German who was returning from the Philippines, where he had been discharged after the war.* He was the only child of his widowed mother, who has a ranch a few miles from here. No one knew he was coming home.

One day the cook belonging to the camp of a construction gang went hunting and came back, running, wild with horror. He had found the body of a man. The coroner and the sheriff were notified, and next morning went out for the body. The wolves had almost destroyed it. High up in a willow, under which the poor man had lain down to die, they saw a small bundle tied in a red bandanna. They found a letter addressed to whoever should find it, saying that the body was that of Benny Louderer. [It gave] them directions how to spare his poor old mother the awful knowledge of how he died. Also

*The Spanish-American War (1898)

32

there was a letter to his mother asking her not to grieve for him and to keep their days faithfully. "Their days," I afterward learned, were anniversaries which they had always kept. [Now his mother would add] "Benny's day."

To this day Mrs. Louderer thinks her boy died of some fever while yet aboard the transport. The manner of his death has been kept so secret that I am the only one who has heard it.

I was so sorry for the poor mother that I resolved to visit her the first opportunity I had. So a few days later I took Jerrine and rode over to the Louderer ranch. It happened to be "Benny's day" that I blundered in upon. I found her to be a dear old German woman living all alone. She had been weeping for hours when I got there, but she had a real feast prepared, although no one had been bidden. She says that God always sends her guests.

She is such a dear old lady! She made us so welcome and she is so entertaining. And then our feast. We had goose and it was *so* delicious. We sat talking until far into the night, and she asked me how I was going to spend Christmas. I told her, "Probably in being homesick." She said that would never do and suggested that we spend it together. She said that the only happiness left her was in making someone else happy. So she had thought of cooking some nice things and going to as many sheep camps as she could, taking with her the good things to the poor exiles, the sheep-herders. I liked the plan and was glad to agree.

Two days before Christmas I had a chance to go down to Mrs. Louderer's in a buggy, so we went. We found her up to her ears in cooking, and such sights and smells I could never describe. Mrs. Louderer had sent a man out several days before to find out how many camps there were and where they were located. There were twelve camps and that means twenty-four men. We roasted six geese, boiled three small hams and three hens. We had besides several meat-loaves and links of sausage. We had twelve large loaves of the best rye bread; a small tub of doughnuts; twelve coffee-cakes, more to be called fruit-cakes, and also a quantity of little cakes with seeds, nuts, and fruit in them. These had a thick coat of icing, some brown, some pink, some white. I had thirteen pounds of butter and six pint jars of jelly, so we melted the jelly and poured it into twelve glasses.

The plan was, to start real early Christmas Eve morning, make our circuit of camps, and wind up the day at Mrs. O'Shaughnessy's to spend the night. Before it was day the man came to feed and to get our horses ready. The man had four horses harnessed and hitched to the sled, on which was placed a wagon-box filled with straw, hot rocks, and blankets. Our twelve boxes were lifted in and tied firmly into place. Then we clambered in and away we went. We didn't follow any road either, but went sweeping across country. We went careening along hillsides with-out even slacking the trot. Luck was with us. I hardly expected to get through with my head unbroken, but not even a glass was cracked.

We found Mrs. Louderer up to her ears in cooking, and such sights and smells I could never describe.

It would have done your heart good to see the sheep-men. They were all delighted, and when you consider that they live solely on canned corn and tomatoes, beans, salt pork, and coffee, you can fancy what they thought of their treat.

Then we turned our faces toward Mrs. O'Shaughnessy's, and got there just in time for supper. Mrs. O'Shaughnessy is a widow, too, and has quite an interesting story. She is a dumpy little woman whose small nose seems to be smelling the stars, it is so tip-tilted. She has the merriest blue eyes and the quickest wit. It is really worth a severe bumping just to be welcomed by her.

We had a late breakfast Christmas morning, but before we were through Mr. Stewart came. It was almost one o'clock when we got home, but all hands helped and I had plenty cooked anyway, so we soon had a good dinner on the table. Mr. Stewart had prepared a Christmas box for Jerrine and me. For me in the box were two dresses, that is, the material to make them. One is a brown and red checked, and the other green [with a] white fleck. For Jerrine there was a pair of shoes and stockings, both stockings full of candy and nuts. He is very bluff in manner, but he is really the kindest person.

Mrs. Louderer stayed until New Year's day. My Christmas was really a very happy one.

Your Friend,
Elinore Rupert

P.S. . . . An interesting day on this ranch is the day the cattle are named. If Mr. Stewart had children he would as soon think of leaving them unnamed as to let a "beastie" go without a name.

On the day they were vaccinated he came into the kitchen and told me he would need me to help him name the "critters." So he and I took turns naming the calves. As fast as a calf was vaccinated it was run out of the chute and he or I called out a name for it and it was booked that way.

The first two he named were the "Duke of Monmouth" and the "Duke of Montrose." I called my first "Oliver Cromwell" and "John Fox." The poor "Mon" had to have revenge, so the next ugly, scrawny little beast he called the "Poop of Rome." And it was a heifer calf, too.

We have a swell lot of names, but I am not sure I could tell you which is "Bloody Mary," or which is "Elizabeth," or indeed, which is which of any of them.

A Confession

April 5, 1910

Dear Mrs. Coney, —

My house joins on to Mr. Stewart's house. It was built that way so that I could "hold down" my land and job at the same time. I see the wisdom of it now, though at first I did not want it that way. My boundary lines run within two feet of Mr. Stewart's house, so it was quite easy to build on.

I think the Patterson's ranch is about twenty-five miles from us. I am glad to tell you they are doing splendidly. Gale is just as thrifty as she can be and Bobby is steady and making money fast. Their baby is the dearest little thing.

I have not treated you quite frankly about something you had a right to know about. I am ashamed and I regret very much that I have not told you. I so dread the possibility of losing your friendship that I will never tell you unless you promise me beforehand to forgive me. Won't you make it easy to "fess" so I may be happy again?

Truly your friend,
Elinore Rupert

June 16, 1910

My Dear Friend, —

Your card just to hand. I wrote you some time ago telling you I had a confession to make and have had no letter since, so thought perhaps you were scared I had done something too bad to forgive. I am suffering just now from eye-strain and can't see to write long at a time, but I reckon I had better confess and get it done with.

The thing I have done is to marry Mr. Stewart. It was such an inconsistent thing to do that I was ashamed to tell you.

I hope my eyes will be better soon and then I will write you a long letter.

Your old friend with a new name,
Elinore Stewart

August 15, 1910

Dear Mrs. Coney, —

    I have been a very busy woman since I began this letter to you several days ago. A dear little child has joined the angels. I dressed him and helped to make his casket. There is no minister in this whole country and I could not bear the little broken lily-bud to be just carted away and buried. So I arranged the funeral and conducted the services. I know I am unworthy and in no way fitted for such a mission, but I did my poor best, and if no one else is comforted, I am.

Your sincere friend,
Elinore Rupert Stewart

Zebbie's Story

Dear Mrs. Coney, —

[Mrs. O'Shaughnessy and I] were down at the barn looking at some new pigs, when we heard the big corral gates swing shut, so we hastened out to see who it could be so late in the day.

It was Zebbie [Zebulon Pike Parker]. He had come on the stage to Burnt Fork and the driver had brought him on here. . . . There was so much to tell, and he whispered he had something to tell me privately, but that he was too tired then. So after supper I hustled him off to bed.

Next morning . . . the men went off to their work and Zebbie and I were left to tell secrets. When he was sure we were alone he took from his trunk a long, flat box. Inside was the most wonderful shirt I have ever seen; it looked like a cross between a night-shirt and a shirt-waist. It was of homespun linen. The bosom was ruffled and tucked, all done by hand, — such tiny stitches, such patience and skill. Then he handed me an old daguerreotype. I unfastened the little golden hook and inside was a face good to see and to remember. The sweet, elusive smile — I couldn't tell where it was, whether it was the mouth or the beautiful eyes that were smiling. Under the glass on the other side was a strand of faded hair and a slip of paper. The writing on the paper was so faded it was scarcely readable, but it said, "Pauline Gorley, age 22, 1860."

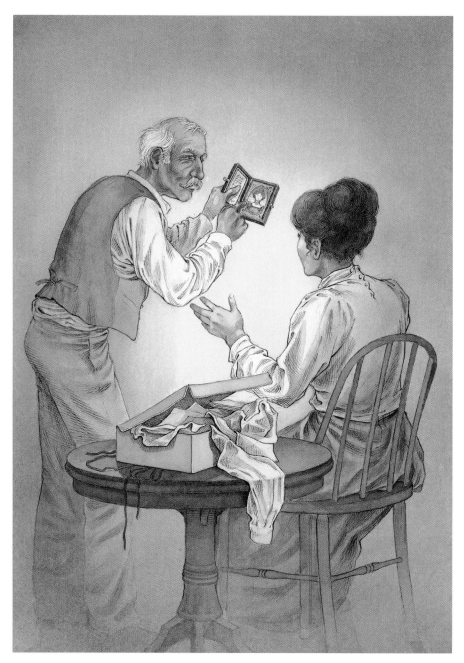

"She was just like the pink hollyhocks that grew by Mother's window."

Next he showed me a note written by Pauline, simply worded, but it held a world of meaning for Zebbie. It said, "I spun and wove this cloth at Adeline's, enough for me a dress and you a shirt, which I made. It is for the wedding, else to be buried in. Yours, Pauline." The shirt, the picture, and the note had waited for him all these years in his sister's care. And now I will tell you the story.

Long, long ago someone did something to some one else and started a feud. Unfortunately the Gorleys were on one side and the Parkers on the other. A Gorley must hate a Parker always, as also a Parker must hate a Gorley. Pauline was the only girl, and she had a regiment of big brothers who gloried in the warfare and wanted only the slightest pretext to shoot a Parker.

[Zebbie] remembers her so perfectly and describes her so plainly that I can picture her easily. She had brown eyes and hair. She wore a pink calico sunbonnet, and Zebbie says "she was just like the pink hollyhocks that grew by Mother's window." Isn't that a sweet picture?

Zebbie had never dared speak to her until one day he had driven over with his mother and sisters to a dinner given on a neighboring plantation. He was standing outside near the wall, when some one dropped a spray of apple blossoms down upon him from an upper window. He looked up and Pauline was leaning out smiling at him. After that he made it a point to frequent places where he might expect her. Finally Zebbie got tired of waiting, and one day he boldly rode up to the Gorley home and formally asked for Pauline's hand. The bullet he got kept him from going to the war with his father and brother when they marched away.

Some time later George Gorley was shot and killed from ambush. Although Zebbie had not yet left his bed the Gorleys believed he did it. One night Pauline came through a heavy rainstorm to warn Zebbie and to beg him, for her sake, to get away as fast as he could that night.

Well, he did as she wished and they never saw each other again. He never went home again until last Thanksgiving, and dear little Pauline had been dead for years. She herself had taken her little gifts for Zebbie to his sister to keep for him. Some years later she died and was buried in the dress she mentioned.

Well, Mrs. O'Shaughnessy returned, and early one morning we [Zebbie, Mrs. O'Shaughnessy, Elinore, and Jerrine] started with a wagon and a bulging mess-box for Zebbie's home. Dandelions spread a carpet of gold. Larkspur grew waist-high with its long spikes of blue. Meadowlarks and robins and bluebirds twittered and sang from every branch, it almost seemed. A sky of tenderest blue bent over us and fleecy little clouds drifted lazily across.

A more delighted man than Zebbie I never saw when we finally drove up to his low, comfortable cabin. The hounds sprang upon him and expressed their joy unmistakably. He went at once to the corrals to see the "critters," and every one of them was safely penned for the night. We went into the cabin and left him fondling the "critters."

Gavotte [the Frenchman taking care of Zebbie's place] did himself proud getting supper. We had trout and the most delicious biscuit. Each of us had a crisp, tender head of lettuce with a spoonful of potato salad in the center. We had preserves made from canned peaches, and the firmest yellow butter.

When supper was over . . . we heard the deep roaring of [a] coming storm, and Zebbie called the hounds in and secured the door. The sparks began to fly up the chimney. Jerrine lay on a bearskin before the fire, and Mrs. O'Shaughnessy and I sat on the old blue "settle" at one side. Gavotte lay on the other side of the fire on the floor, his hands under his head. Zebbie got out his beloved old fiddle, tuned up, and began playing. Outside the storm was raging, growing worse all the time. Zebbie played and played. The worse the tumult, the harder the storm, the harder he played. I verily believe we were all bewitched. I shouldn't have been surprised to have seen witches and gnomes come tumbling down the chimney or flying in at the door, riding on the crest of the storm. . . .

Elinore Stewart

The Horse Thieves

Dear Mrs. Coney,—

Mrs. Louderer had come over to see our boy. Together we had prepared supper and were waiting for Clyde, who had gone to the post-office. Soon he came, and we had supper. Then they began their inevitable game of cribbage, while I sat near the fire with Baby on my lap. Clyde was telling us of a raid on a ranch about seventy-five miles away, in which the thieves had driven off thirty head of fine horses. There were only two of the thieves, and the sheriff with a large posse was pursuing them. We were in no way alarmed. The trouble was all in the next county, and somehow that always seems so far away.

Jerrine was enjoying the pictures in a paper illustrating early days on the range, wild scenes of roping and branding. I remarked that I didn't believe there were any more such times. Mrs. Louderer replied, "Dot yust shows how much it iss you do not know. You shall come to mine house and when away you come it shall be wiser as when you left." A little trip seemed the most desirable thing I could think of.

[The next morning] we jogged along right merrily. Prosperous little ranches dotted the view, ripening grain rustled pleasantly in the warm morning sunshine. The

46

quaking aspens were just beginning to turn yellow; everywhere purple asters were a blaze of glory. Over it all the sky was so deeply blue, with little, airy, white clouds drifting lazily along. All was so peaceful that horse thieves and desperate men seemed too remote to think about.

Presently we crossed the creek and headed our course due north toward the desert and the buttes. I asked [Mrs. Louderer] where we were supposed to be going. "We iss going to the mouth of Dry Creek by, where it goes Black's Fork into. Dere mine punchers holdts five huntert steers. We shall de camp visit and you shall come back wiser as when you went."

We had entered the desert by noon; the warm, red sands fell away from the wheels with soft, hissing sounds. Occasionally a little horned toad sped panting along before us, suddenly darting aside to watch with bright, cunning eyes as we passed. Some one had placed a buffalo's skull beside a big bunch of sage and on the sage a splendid pair of elk's antlers. We saw many such scattered over the sands, grim reminders of a past forever gone.

The camp was quite near the river so as to be handy to water and to have the willows for wood. When the regular supper-time arrived the punchers began to gather in, and the "boss," who had been to town about some business, came in and brought back the news of the man-hunt. The punchers sat about the fire, eating hungrily from their tin plates and eagerly listening to the recital. Two of the boys were tenderfeet: one from Tennessee called "Daisy Belle," because he whistled that tune so much and because he had

WHERE THE BUFFALO ROAM

In 1860, 13 million bison lived on the Great Plains. Twenty-five years later, just a few hundred still survived. What happened?

Plains Indians had hunted buffalo for their meat and hide for thousands of years before Europeans arrived in the Americas. The buffalo provided almost everything the Native Americans needed to stay alive. In the early 1800s, as more and more white hunters killed the great, shaggy-maned beasts, the herds began to diminish. The final death knell was struck during the 1860s and 1870s, when railroads were built across the plains. Professional hunters arrived to supply meat for the crews building the rails.

Special excursion trains offered passengers the chance to shoot buffalo from the comfort and security of a railway car. As thousands of hunters eager for an easy buck or a trophy descended on the plains, entire herds were wiped out. To make matters worse, a new tanning process that turned the hides into expensive leather for the well-to-do encouraged wholesale slaughter. By the time Elinore was homesteading, only one herd of twenty-five bison remained in Wyoming.

In 1905 the American Bison Society was formed. With the help of President Theodore Roosevelt, its members established herds on various public lands. As a result, the buffalo never did become extinct. Today about 500,000 buffalo live in the United States and Canada. More than 2,000 buffalo roam through Wyoming's Yellowstone National Park.

nose-bleed so much. The other [was] "N'Yawk," so called from his native State. N'Yawk was a great boaster. [He] said he wasn't afraid of no durned outlaw — said his father had waded in bloody gore up to his neck and that he was a chip off the old block. [He] rather hoped the chase would come our way so he could try his marksmanship.

The air began to grow chill and the sky was becoming overcast. Preparations for the night busied everybody. Some poles were set up and a tarpaulin arranged for Mrs. Louderer and me to sleep under. Mrs. Louderer and Jerrine lay down on some blankets and I unrolled some more, which I was glad to notice were clean, for Baby and myself. I can't remember ever being more tired and sleepy, but I couldn't go to sleep. I don't think I was afraid, but I certainly was nervous.

I was in that dozy state, half asleep, when nothing is quite clear, when I was brought suddenly into keen consciousness by a loud voice demanding "Hello! Whose outfit is this?"

"This is the 7 Up — Louderer's," the boss called back. "What's wanted?"

"Is that you, Mat? This is Ward's posse. We been after Meeks and Murdock all night. It's so durned dark we can't see, but we got to keep going. Their horses are about played. We got to search your camp."

"Sure thing," the boss answered. "Hi there, you Herm, fix these fellers something to eat."

We were surrounded. I could hear the clanking of spurs and the sound of the wet, tired horses shaking

We were surrounded. I could hear the clanking of spurs and the sound of the wet, tired horses shaking themselves and rattling the saddles on every side.

themselves and rattling the saddles on every side. The sheriff went from bed to bed with a lantern. He threw back the flap of our tent and flashed the lantern about. The men had gathered about the fire and were gulping hot coffee and cold beef and bread. The rain ran off their slickers in little rivulets. Before they had finished eating we heard a shot, followed by dull booms. The men were in their saddles and gone in less time than it takes to tell it. I kissed my baby's little downy head and went to sleep.

The next I knew, Herman had a tin pan on which he was beating a vigorous tattoo, all the time hollering, "We haf cackle-berries und antelope steak for breakfast." Never having seen a cackle-berry, my imagination pictured them as some very luscious wild fruit. I couldn't wait until the men should eat and be gone, so I surprised them by joining the very earliest about the fire. I held out my tin plate and received some of the steak, an egg, and two delicious biscuits. I finished and told Herman I was ready for my cackle-berries.

"Listen to her now, will you?" he asked. "How many cackle-berries does you want? You haf had so many as I haf cooked for you."

"Why, Herman, I haven't had a single berry," I said.

Then such a roar of laughter. Mr. Watson gently explained to me that eggs and cackle-berries were one and the same.

N'Yawk joined us in a few minutes. "What the deuce was you fellers kicking up such a rumpus fer last night?" he asked.

"You blamed blockhead, don't you know?" the boss answered. "Why, the sheriff searched this camp last night. And durn your sleepy head! You just lay there and snored."

N'Yawk turned to get his breakfast. His light shirt was bloodstained in the back—seemed to be soaked. "What's the matter with your shirt, it's soaked with blood!" someone asked.

"Then that durned Daisy Belle has been crawling in with me, that's all," he said. "Blame his bleeding snoot."

Then Mr. Watson said, "Daisy ain't been in all night." That started an inquiry and search which speedily showed that some one with a bleeding wound had gotten in with N'Yawk. It also developed that Mr. Watson's splendid horse and saddle were gone.

Now all was bustle and excitement. It was plainly evident that one of the outlaws had lain hidden in N'Yawk's bed while the sheriff was there, and that afterwards he had saddled the horse and made his escape. His own horse was found in the willows, the saddle cut loose and the bridle off.

By sun-up the search-party returned, all too worn-out with twenty-four hours in the saddle to continue the hunt. The chase was hopeless anyway, for the search-party had gone north in the night. The wounded outlaw had doubtless heard the sheriff talking and, the coast being clear to the southward, had got the fresh horse and was by that time probably safe in the heavy forests and mountains of Utah. His getting in with N'Yawk had been a daring ruse, but a successful one.

I didn't get to see the branding that was to have taken place on the range that day. The boss insisted on taking the trail of his valued horse. He was very angry.

My own home looked mighty good to me when we drove up that evening. I don't want any more wild life on the range—not for a while, anyway.

Your ex-Washlady,
Elinore Rupert Stewart

The Homesteader's Marriage
and a Little Funeral

December 2, 1912

Dear Mrs. Coney, —

Every time I get a new letter from you I get a new inspiration, and I am always glad to hear from you.

I have often wished I might tell you all about my Clyde, but have not because of two things. One is I could not even begin without telling you what a good man he is, and I didn't want you to think I could do nothing but brag. The other reason is the haste I married in. But although I married in haste, I have no cause to repent. That is very fortunate because I have never had one bit of leisure to repent in. So I am lucky all around.

The engagement was powerfully short because both agreed that the trend of events and ranch work seemed to require that we be married first and do our "sparking" afterward. In Wyoming, ranchers can scarcely take time even to be married in the springtime. That having been settled, the license was sent for by mail. As soon as it came Mr. Stewart saddled Chub and went down to the house of Mr. Pearson, the justice of the peace and a friend of long standing. He told Mr. Pearson he wanted him and his family to come up the following Wednesday.

Well, there was no time to make wedding clothes, so I had to "do up" what I did have. I had brought a beautiful

54

pair of shoes to wear on that day. But my vanity had squeezed my feet a little, so while I was so busy at work I had kept on a worn old pair, intending to put on the new ones later; but when the Pearsons drove up I forgot all about the old shoes and the apron I wore.

I had only been here six weeks then, and I was a stranger. That is why I had no one to help me and was so confused and hurried. As soon as the newcomers were warm, Mr. Stewart told me I had better come over by him and stand up. It was a large room I had to cross, and how I did it before all those strange eyes I never knew. All I can remember very distinctly is hearing Mr. Stewart saying, "I will," and myself chiming in that I would, too. Happening to glance down, I saw that I had forgotten to take off my apron or my old shoes. But just then Mr. Pearson pronounced us man and wife.

I had not thought I should ever marry again. Jerrine was always such a dear little pal, and I wanted to just knock about foot-loose and free to see life as a gypsy sees it. I had planned to see the Cliff-Dwellers' home; to live right there until I caught the spirit of the surroundings enough to live over their lives in imagination anyway. I had planned to see the old missions and to go to Alaska; to hunt in Canada. I even dreamed of Honolulu. Life stretched out before me one long, happy jaunt. I aimed to see all the world I could. But first I wanted to try homesteading.

Do you remember, I wrote you of a little baby boy dying? That was my own little Jamie, our first little son. For a long time my heart was crushed. He was such a sweet, beautiful boy. He died of erysipelas. So you see,

Happening to glance down, I saw that I had forgotten to take off my apron or my old shoes. But just then Mr. Pearson pronounced us man and wife.

our union is sealed by love and welded by a great sorrow.

God has given me two more precious little sons. The old sorrow is not so keen now. I can bear to tell you about it, but I never could before. When you think of me, you must think of me as one who is truly happy.

With much love to you, I am

"Honest and truly" yours,
Elinore Rupert Stewart

The Adventure of the Christmas Tree

January 6, 1913

My Dear Friend,—

I have put off writing you and thanking you for your thought for us until now so that I could tell you of our very happy Christmas and our deer hunt all at once.

To begin with, Mr. Stewart and [Clyde] Junior have gone to Boulder to spend the winter. Clyde wanted his mother to have a chance to enjoy our boy, so, as he had to go, he took Junior with him. Then those of my dear neighbors nearest my heart decided to prevent a lonely Christmas for me. So on December 21st came Mrs. Louderer with an immense plum pudding and a big "wurst." A little later came Mrs. O'Shaughnessy on her frisky pony, Chief.

Well we were getting supper when a great stamping-off of snow proclaimed a newcomer. It was Gavotte, and we were powerfully glad to see him because he would contrive some unusual amusement. He had heard that Clyde was going to have a deer-drive, so he had come down to join the hunt just for the fun. [He] was very much disappointed to find there was going to be no hunt. At last [he] proposed that we have a drive of our own. Two miles away there is a huge mountain called Phillipeco, and deer were said to be plentiful up there. At one time there had been a sawmill on the mountain, and

58

there were a number of deserted cabins in which we could make ourselves comfortable.

Well, we were all astir early the next morning and soon grain, bedding, and chuckbox were in the wagon. Then Mrs. Louderer, the children, and myself piled in; Mrs. O'Shaughnessy bestrode Chief, and Gavotte stalked on ahead to pick our way, and we were off.

It was three o'clock before we reached the old mill camp. Soon we had a roaring fire, and Gavotte made the horses comfortable in one of the cabins. After dark we sat around the fire eating peanuts and listening to Gavotte and Mrs. Louderer telling stories of their different great forests. But soon Gavotte took his big sleeping bag and retired to another cabin, warning us that we must be up early.

It seemed only a short time until someone knocked on our door and we were all wide awake in a minute. It was Gavotte, and he called through a crack saying he had been hearing queer noises for an hour and he was going to investigate. We scrambled into our clothes quickly and ran outdoors to listen.

I can never describe to you the weird beauty of a moonlight night among the pines when the snow is sparkling and gleaming, the deep silence unbroken even by the snapping of a twig. We stood shivering and straining our ears and were about to go back to bed when we heard faintly a long-drawn out wail as if all the suffering and sorrow on earth were bound up in that one sound. We couldn't tell which way it came from; it seemed to vibrate through the air and chill our hearts.

We went in, made up the fire, and sat in silence, wondering what we should see or hear next. After an age, we heard Gavotte crunching through the snow, whistling cheerily to reassure us. He had crossed the canyon to the new mill camp, where he found two women, loggers' wives, and some children. One of the women, he said, was "so very seek." [She was going to have a baby.]

Mrs. Louderer stayed and took care of the children while Mrs. O'Shaughnessy and I followed after Gavotte, panting and stumbling through the snow. At last we reached the ugly clearing where the new camps stood. Gavotte escorted us to the door and then returned to our camp. Entering, we saw the poor, little soon-to-be-mother huddled on her poor bed, while an older woman stood nearby.

Secretly, I felt it all to be a big nuisance to be dragged out from my warm, comfortable bed to traipse through the snow at that time of the night. But the moment poor little Molly spoke I was glad I was living, because she was a poor little Southern girl. Her husband had been sent on a mission to Alabama, and the poor girl had fallen in love with his handsome face, so she had run away with him. But now she said she knew her husband was dead because he and the other woman's husband had gone two weeks before to get their summer's wages and buy supplies. Neither man had come back, so they believed the men to be frozen somewhere on the road.

Well, we had the water hot and had filled some bottles and placed them around our patient, and after a couple of hours the tiny little stranger came into the world. It had been necessary to have a great fire in order to have light,

60

so as soon as we got baby dressed I opened the door a little to cool the room and Molly saw the morning star twinkling merrily. "Oh," she said, "that is what I will call my little girlie—Star, dear little Star."

It is strange, isn't it? How our spirits will revive after some great ordeal. Molly had been sure she was going to die and saw nothing to live for. Now that she had had a cup of hot milk and held her red little baby close, she was just as happy and hopeful as if she had never left her best friends and home to follow the uncertain fortunes of young Will Crosby.

Soon day was abroad, and we went outdoors for a fresh breath. The other woman invited us into her cabin, and oh, the little [children] were everywhere, poor, half-clad little things! Some sour-dough biscuit and a can of condensed milk was everything they had to eat.

Just then two shots rang out in quick succession, and soon Gavotte came staggering along with a deer across his shoulders. That he left for the family. Leaving the woman to dress the venison with her oldest boy's aid, we put out across the canyon for our own breakfast. In a short time we were rolling homeward.

Gavotte knew the two loggers were in Green River and were then at work storing ice for the railroad. The men actually had got drunk, lost their money, and were then trying to replace it. After we debated a bit we decided we could not enjoy Christmas with those people in want up there in the cold. Then we got busy. You should have seen us! Every odd garment that had ever been left by men who have worked here was hauled out, and Mrs.

O'Shaughnessy's deft fingers soon had a pile of garments cut.

All next day we sewed as hard as we could, and Gavotte cooked as hard as he could. He asked for all the bright paper we could find. He made gorgeous birds, butterflies, and flowers out of paper that once wrapped parcels. Than he asked us for some silk thread, but I had none, so he told us to comb our hair and give him the combings. We did, and with a drop of mucilage he would fasten a hair to a bird's back and then hold it up by the hair. At a few feet's distance it looked exactly as though the bird was flying. We had a lot of fun shaping and coloring candies. Mrs. Louderer cut up her big plum pudding and put it into a dozen small bags. These Gavotte carefully covered with green paper. I never had so much fun in my life as I had preparing for that Christmas.

At ten o'clock, the morning of the 24th, we were again on our way up the mountainside. We had dinner at the old camp, and then Gavotte hunted us a way out to the new, and we smuggled our things into Molly's cabin so the children should have a real surprise. They paid no attention when he cut a small tree. The children were sent to the spring to water the horses and they were all allowed to ride, so that took them out of the way while Gavotte nailed the tree into a box he had filled with dirt to hold it steady.

It was the work of a few moments to get the tree ready, and it was the most beautiful one I ever saw. Your largest bell, dear Mrs. Coney, dangled from the topmost branch. The hairs that held the birds and butterflies could not be seen, and the effect was beautiful. We had a bucket

He made gorgeous birds, butterflies, and flowers out of paper that once wrapped parcels.

of apples rubbed bright, and these we fastened to the tree. The puddings looked pretty too, and we had done up the parcels that held the clothes as attractively as we could. We saved the candy and the peanuts to put in their little stockings.

As soon as it was dark we lighted the candles and then their mother called the children. Oh, if you could have seen them! It was the very first Christmas tree they had ever seen and they didn't know what to do. The very first present Gavotte handed out was a pair of trousers for eight-year-old Brig, but he just stood and stared at the tree.

After the presents had all been distributed we put the phonograph on a box and had a dandy concert. We played "There Were Shepherds," "Ave Maria," and "Sweet Christmas Bells." Our concert lasted two hours. By that time the little fellows were so sleepy that they were put to bed, but they hung up their stockings first, and even Molly hung hers up too. We filled them with peanuts and candy.

Next morning the happiness broke out in new spots. The mother was radiantly thankful for a warm petticoat; that it was made of a blanket too small for a bed didn't bother her. Molly openly rejoiced in her new gown, and that it was made of ugly gray flannel she didn't care. Baby Star Crosby looked perfectly sweet in her little new clothes. And so it was about everything. We all got so much out of so little. I will never again allow even the smallest thing to go to waste. There was never anything more true than that it is more blessed to give than to receive.

CHILDREN IN THE WEST

Childhood was a precarious time in the West. Nearly all families lost at least one child to illness or injury. In those days before antibiotics or most preventive vaccinations, children could die from childhood diseases such as measles or infections such as erysipelas, as little Jamie Stewart did. They could fall prey to snakebite, wild animals, and all kinds of accidents.

Children might be an extra responsibility, but they were also an invaluable source of help. On a ranch, every pair of hands was needed. Youngsters gathered eggs, fed chickens, milked cows, fetched water, and planted gardens. When they were older, they did household chores and plowed, planted, and tended livestock. Every farming or ranching family was a team, and children were valued members.

Despite its dangers, the West could be a wonderful place to grow up. The wide-open country was like one huge backyard. Children went swimming in local water holes and camping in the mountains. Frontier families took every opportunity to get together, at christenings and burials, birthdays, anniversaries, and holidays. Western towns offered traveling circuses and variety shows. The most magical time of the year was Christmas. After cutting down an evergreen in a neighboring woods, families would decorate it with paper animals, popcorn strings, and candles in tin holders. Stockings were hung over the fireplace and stuffed with oranges and peppermint and gingersnaps. There were warm new clothes for all—and for the very lucky child, a store-bought doll or drum.

It was just dusk when we reached home. Away off on a bare hill a wolf barked. A big owl hooted lonesomely among the pines, and soon a pack of yelping coyotes went scampering across the frozen waste.

It was not the Christmas I had in mind, but it was a *dandy* one, just the same.

With best wishes for you for a happy, *happy* New Year,

Sincerely your friend,
Elinore Rupert Stewart

The Joys of Homesteading

January 23, 1913

Dear Mrs. Coney.—

When I read of the hard times among the Denver poor, I feel like urging them every one to get out and file on land. To me, homesteading is the solution of all poverty's problems. But I do realize that temperament has much to do with success in any undertaking, and persons afraid of coyotes and work and loneliness had better let ranching alone. At the same time, any woman who can stand her own company, can see the beauty of the sunset, loves growing things, and is willing to put in as much time at careful labor as she does over the washtub will certainly succeed; will have independence, plenty to eat all the time, and a home of her own in the end.

You'd think I wanted you to homestead, wouldn't you! But I am only thinking of the troops of tired, worried women, sometimes even cold and hungry, scared to death of losing their places [at] work, who could have plenty to eat, who could have good fires by gathering the wood, and comfortable homes of their own, if they but had the courage and determination to get them.

With much love to you from Jerrine and myself, I am

Yours affectionately,
Elinore Rupert Stewart

The Efficient Mrs. O'Shaughnessy

May 5, 1913

Dear Mrs. Coney, —

Your letter of April 25 certainly was a surprise, but a very welcome one. We are so rushed with spring work that we don't even go to the office for the mail, and I owe you letters and thanks.

Little Star Crosby is growing to be the sweetest little kid. I am afraid you give me too much credit for being of help to poor little Molly. It was Mrs. O'Shaughnessy who was the real help. She is a woman of great courage and decision and of splendid sense and judgment.

A few days ago a man she had working for her got his finger-nail mashed off and neglected to care for it. Mrs. O'Shaughnessy examined it and found that gangrene had set in. She didn't tell him, but made various preparations and then told him she had heard that if there was danger of blood-poisoning it would show if the finger was placed on wood and the patient looked toward the sun. So the man placed his finger on the chopping block and before he could bat his eye she had chopped off the black, swollen finger. It was so sudden and unexpected that there seemed to be no pain.

Then Mrs. O'Shaughnessy showed him the green streak already starting up his arm. The man seemed dazed

FRONTIER MEDICINE

In the wide-open spaces of the West, doctors were few and far between. It fell to the woman of the ranch to take care of her family and the hired help. When Elinore was in Denver, she went to Dr. Theresa Fantz to be treated for "la grippe," the flu. But in Burntfork it was up to her to nurse her husband when he got sick. "Out here where we can get no physician we have to dope ourselves," she told Mrs. Coney when Clyde fell ill. "So that I had to be house-keeper, nurse, doctor, and general overseer."

When Mrs. O'Shaughnessy's ranch hand developed a gan-grenous finger, the nearest doctor was forty-five miles away. Luckily she knew just what to do—and saved his life. Chopping off a finger was all in a day's work for the resourceful woman rancher.

Women were lucky if a midwife or neighbor was nearby to assist at childbirth. When Elinore gave birth to her third boy, the hired girl who was supposed to help her decided to elope! Elinore had to depend on her husband instead. Afterward, he said he felt too weak to wash and dress the baby. So Elinore had to do it herself.

and she was afraid of shock, so she gave him a dose of morphine and whiskey. Then with a quick stroke of the razor she laid open the green streak and immersed the whole arm in a strong solution of bichloride of mercury for twenty minutes. She then dressed the wound with absorbent cotton saturated with olive oil and carbolic acid, bundled her patient into a buggy, and drove forty-five miles that night to get him to a doctor. The doctor told us that only her quick action and knowledge of what to do saved the man's life.

Very truly your friend,
Elinore Rupert Stewart

How It Happened

Dear Mrs. Coney, —

Your letter of the 8th to hand, and in order to catch you before you leave I'll answer at once and not wait for time. I always think I shall do better with more time, but with three "bairns," garden, chickens, cows, and housework I don't seem to find much time for anything. Indeed, I am glad to tell you how I happened to meet the "gude mon" [her husband, Clyde].

It all happened because I had a stitch in my side. After Dr. F. punched and prodded, she said, "Why, you have the grippe." Rev. Father Corrigan had been preparing me to take the Civil Service examination, and that afternoon a lesson was due, so I went over to let him see how little I knew. I was in pain and was so blue that I could hardly speak without weeping, so I told the Reverend Father how tired I was of the rattle and bang [of the city of Denver], of the glare and the soot, the smells and the hurry. I told him what I longed for was the sweet, free open, and that I would like to homestead. That was Saturday evening. He advised me to go straight uptown and put an ad in the paper, so as to get it into the Sunday paper. I did so, and because I wanted as much rest and quiet as possible I took Jerrine and went uptown and got a nice quiet room.

On the following Wednesday I received a letter from Clyde, who was in Boulder visiting his mother. He was leaving for Wyoming the following Saturday and wanted an interview, if his proposition suited me. I was so glad of his offer, but at the same time I couldn't know what kind of person he was. So, to lessen any risk, I asked him to come to the Sunshine Mission, where Miss Ryan was going to help me "size him up." He didn't know that part of it, of course, but he stood inspection admirably. I am as proud and happy today as I was the day that I became his wife.

Junior can talk quite well, and even Calvin jabbers. The children are all well, and Jerrine writes a little every day to you.

I do hope you will have a very happy summer, and that you will share your happiness with me in occasional letters.

With much love,
Elinore Stewart

P.S. IN WRITING I FORGOT TO SAY THAT THE REVEREND FATHER THOUGHT IT A GOOD PLAN TO GET A POSITION AS HOUSEKEEPER FOR SOME RANCHER WHO WOULD ADVISE ME ABOUT LAND AND WATER RIGHTS. BY KEEPING HOUSE, HE POINTED OUT, I COULD HAVE A HOME AND A LIVING AND AT THE SAME TIME SEE WHAT KIND OF A HOMESTEAD I COULD GET.

Success

November, 1913

Dear Mrs. Coney, —

This is Sunday and I suppose I ought not to be writing, but I must write to you and I may not have another chance soon.

Now, this is the letter I have been wanting to write you for a long time, but could not because until now I had not actually proven all I wanted to prove. Perhaps it will not interest you, but if you see a woman who wanted to homestead and is a little afraid she will starve, you can tell her what I am telling you.

I never did like to theorize, and so this year I set out to prove that a woman could ranch if she wanted to. We like to grow potatoes on new ground, that is, newly cleared land on which no crop has been grown. Few weeds grow on new land, so it makes less work. So I selected my potato patch, and the man ploughed it, although I could have done that if Clyde would have let me. I cut the potatoes, Jerrine helped, and we dropped them in the rows. The man covered them, and that ends the man's part. By that time the garden ground was ready, so I planted the garden. I had almost an acre in vegetables. I irrigated and I cultivated it myself.

We had all the vegetables we could possibly use, and now Jerrine and I have put in our cellar full, and this is

73

what we have: One large bin of potatoes (more than two tons), half a ton of carrots, a large bin of beets, one of turnips, one of onions, one of parsnips, and on the other side of the cellar we have more than one hundred heads of cabbage. I have experimented and found a kind of squash that can be raised here. And also I raised lots of green tomatoes, and as we like them preserved, I made them all up that way.

I milked ten cows twice a day all summer; have sold enough butter to pay for a year's supply of flour and gasoline. We use a gasoline lamp. I have raised enough chickens to completely renew my flock, and all we wanted to eat, and have some fryers to go into the winter with. I have enough turkeys for all of our birthdays and holidays.

I raised a great many flowers and I worked several days in the field. In all I have told about I have had no help but Jerrine. Clyde's mother spends each summer with us, and she helped me with the cooking and the babies. Many of my neighbors did better than I did, although I know many town people would doubt my doing so much, but I did it. I have tried every kind of work this ranch affords, and I can do any of it. Of course I *am* extra strong, but those who try know that strength and knowledge come with doing. I just love to experiment, to work, and to prove out things, so that ranch life and "roughing it" just suit me.

The End

Editor's Note

Elinore Stewart was an engaging and plain-spoken writer. Her style is easily accessible to most readers. In editing her letters, I have sometimes shortened sentences for ease of meaning. However, every word in this book is Elinore's own, except for an occasional linking word or phrase, which I have placed in brackets.

The text is from the 1914 Houghton Mifflin edition of *Letters of a Woman Homesteader* and has been abridged for young people.

Glossary

Babes in the Woods a popular nineteenth-century tale about two lost children

bairn child

butte a flat-topped mountain with steep sides

Cliff Dwellers prehistoric Native Americans who built their homes in cliff walls

daguerreotype an early form of photograph, often set in a decorative case and closed with a small hook

Duke of Monmouth and **Duke of Montrose** Scottish noblemen

erysipelas skin infection accompanied by fever

file to record a claim

gangrene the death of soft tissue

heifer female calf

la grippe the flu

morphine a painkiller

mucilage glue

Navajos blankets

Plymouth Rocks hens

Poop of Rome the pope

puncher cowpuncher, or cowboy

round-up herding cattle together

snoot nose

tarpaulin waterproofed canvas

tenderfoot inexperienced newcomer

To Learn More About Ranching and Homesteading

Books
Nonfiction

Freedman, Russell. *Buffalo Hunt*. New York: Holiday House, 1988.

———. *Children of the Wild West*. New York: Clarion Books, 1983.

———. *Cowboys of the Wild West*. New York: Clarion Books, 1985.

Lauber, Patricia. *Cowboys and Cattle Ranching: Yesterday and Today*. New York: Thomas Y. Crowell, 1973.

Miller, Brandon Marie. *Buffalo Gals: Women of the Old West*. Minneapolis, MN: Lerner Publications, 1995.

Stefoff, Rebecca. *American Voices from the Opening of the West*. New York: Marshall Cavendish, 2003.

———. *Women Pioneers*. New York: Facts on File, 1995.

Wade, Mary Dodson. *Homesteading on the Plains: Daily Life in the Land of Laura Ingalls Wilder*. Brookfield, CT: Millbrook Press, 1997.

Historical Fiction

Cushman, Karen. *The Ballad of Lucy Whipple*. New York: Clarion Books, 1996.

Gregory, Kristiana. *Across the Wide and Lonesome Prairie*. New York: Scholastic, 1997.

Websites*

For information about women in the West:
www.womenshistory.about.com/cs/westernamerica

For links to other sites on women in the West:
www.over-land.com

Wyoming Home Page
www.state.wy.us

Burntfork Home Page:
www.burntforkwyoming.com

* Websites change from time to time. For additional online information, check with the media specialist at your local library.

About the Editor

Ruth Ashby was educated at Yale University and the University of Virginia, where she taught women's studies and literature. She is the author of more than twenty books for young people, among them *Herstory* (Viking, 1995), *Elizabethan England* (Benchmark Books, 1999), *Victorian England* (Benchmark Books, 2003), and *Around the World in 1800* (Benchmark Books, 2003). She lives with her family on Long Island, New York, and teaches English at a nearby college when she is not writing and editing books.

Index

Page numbers for illustrations are in **boldface.**